T C WILDS'

Royal Albert China

A Victorian Pottery - 3

No. 3 in a series by Peter Beckett

Published by Peter Beckett.
Telephone: 01782 343838

Commissioned by Ellis Bevan
67 The Strand, Longton, Stoke-on-Trent, ST3 2NS
Tel/Fax: 01782 312178

ISBN 0-9546394-1-3

By the same author:

'A Victorian Pottery, Thos. Foresters' - The Forgotten Giant'

Published by: Three Counties Publishing (Books) Ltd,
PO Box 435, Leek, Staffordshire.

'A Victorian Pottery - 2. The History of Royal Stafford & Gladstone China'

Published by: Peter Beckett.
Telephone: 01782 343838

ROYAL ALBERT
Bone China
OLD COUNTRY ROSES
THOS. C. WILD & SONS LTD · LONGTON · STOKE-ON-TRENT · STAFFS

Contents

Acknowledgments

Firstly, many thanks to Ellis Bevan for commissioning this book and giving me the chance to tell the story of this famous potter.

I would like to thank my son-in-law Mr. Justin Heath for his time and patience in checking and correcting my original manuscript.

Thanks to Mr. Roger Pitts for his hospitality and the help he gave me in regard to the latter years of T C Wild and his family.

Thanks also to Angela Lee of the Gladstone Pottery Museum.

And last but not least, a big thank you to Tableware International, for allowing me to use so many photos from their periodicals, *The Pottery Gazette, and Pottery Gazette and Glass Trade Review.*

Foreword

The history of the T C Wild group of companies, which includes such famous pottery names as 'Chapmans', 'Roslyn China', 'Shore & Coggins' etc., is really the history of the man himself - Thomas Clarke Wild.

And the history of 'TC' reads more like fiction than fact!

As one of nine children born to Tom and Clara Wild of Normacot, Stoke-on-Trent, young Thomas was sent out to work as a 'jigger - turner' (a demeaning, soul-destroying job), in one of the local pottery factories at the tender age of ***eight*........fifty years later, he was not only a millionaire, but had control over twelve large pottery manufacturers, employing more than two thousand workers. He was also Stoke-on-Trent's very first Lord Mayor.

The story of the *products* made by T C Wild, most notably *'Royal Albert Bone China'*, is just as dramatic. Begun in 1895, in an old run-down pot-bank, '*Royal Albert Crown China*, as it was first called, would, less than forty years on, become a world leader in 'fine bone china', with record export sales to every corner of the globe.

In the following pages I have tried to chronicle, not only the history of T C Wild himself, but also the products, factories and characters that made up this huge empire that he created in Longton, Stoke-on-Trent, in the first half of the twentieth century.

Peter Beckett

Chapter One

A Sign of Things to Come

In 1896, there was an article in the *'Pottery Gazette'* describing each of the six towns that go to make up 'The Potteries'. This is a little of what they had to say at the time about Longton, the most southerly of the Pottery towns.

"At present, the visitor on arriving at the market-place will be struck by nothing in particular, unless it is the dinginess of the railway station, and the similarity in this respect of the other visible buildings. This is due chiefly to the smoke, and as it cannot be avoided, the visitor had better make up his mind to it, and get to business....

"As he passes up Stafford or Market Street, he will pass more china factories than he can remember the names of, and if he passes any of the proprietors thereof, he will notice that they seem fairly alive, and bear an aspect of being pretty well satisfied with themselves....

"The works are not generally models of elegance or even convenience, but are much better than they used to be, and many of them have been rebuilt and leave nothing to be desired. There are

about ninety pot-works in Longton, about three quarters of which are china works, and the rest earthenware of various kinds.

"But the character of a town depends upon its people more than upon its buildings, and the people of Longton are sui generis - *they are Longtonians. The Longton manufacturer is mostly a self-made man, who by dint of a certain practical aptitude has graduated from the work-bench to the master's office. It is this peculiar practicalness which is the distinguishing feature of Longton."*

Although the description 'self-made man' might have applied to quite a number of the nineteenth century pottery manufacturers in Longton, history records that there was one man in particular who stood head and shoulders above the rest. A man who had started his working life at eight years of age as a 'jigger-turner', one of the most demeaning and laborious jobs on a pot-bank, yet who worked his way up with such energy and tenacity, that by the time he was sixty he had controlling interests in more than a dozen different factories (which together employed in excess of two thousand workers) and who, when he died in the nineteen thirties, left an estate worth over a million pounds at today's value (2004).

This was Thomas Clarke Wild, or T C as he was known throughout the Potteries, and in 1896 when the above article was published, he had just started out to build his empire.

Thomas Clarke Wild

Born on the 11th of September 1864, Thomas Clarke Wild was the second of nine children born to Mr and Mrs Thos. Wild of Beaconsfield Villas, Normacot. And although the family was not exactly 'on the bread-line' (his father owned a small grocer's shop, and had a modest interest in a local pot-bank) being part of such a large family (four brothers and four sisters), it was important that as soon as he was old enough, young Thomas should contribute to the household's expenses.

Thus it was that young Thomas started work at the age of eight and a half, in the factory his father was involved with - Beck, Wild and Co`s Beaconsfield Pottery, Anchor Road, Longton.

He was employed as a 'jigger-turner', an awful, soul destroying job which involved continually turning a wooden handle which operated, via an endless leather belt, the jigger, or whirler, on which the flat-ware (i.e. saucers, plates etc.) was formed by the 'flat-maker' (see photo). It was very important to the flat-maker that the jigger was turned at a constant speed, any deviation could cause him to spoil the article he was making, so woe betide the turner if he should slow down or speed up - he would probably get the remains of the spoiled ware about his ears. And as the flat-maker was paid by the piece (i.e. he was only paid for the ware that he made), there would be little or no respite for young Thomas.

Jigger Turner

Thomas, being so young, was employed as a 'part-timer' at the factory, his hours being from six o'clock in the morning, to one o'clock in the afternoon - *seven hours* (not exactly what one would call part-time in today's workplace). For this he was paid the princely sum of one shilling (5p) per week.

In the afternoon, after a hurried lunch, he would make his way down to St. James` school in School Lane, Longton where, for 2d (1p) a week, he was taught the three R's.

St. James' School (2004)

* * *

In the late nineteenth century, very few houses in Normacot had the luxury of piped water; all the water needed for drinking or cooking would have had to be fetched from a nearby pump or well, or better still, from one of the local springs that delivered clean sweet water (all since dried up, but commemorated in some of the street names - Spring Road, Upper Spring Road, Watery Lane etc.).

Thomas, displaying a keen sense of initiative even at this early age, realised that there was money to be made here. So, after school had finished in the evening, he could be spotted with a bucket in each hand, delivering spring water to the local residents for a few coppers at a time.

This trait of always being on the look-out for ways of making money, coupled with his enormous energy and drive, would eventually help to make Thomas Clarke Wild, one of the leading industrialists in North Staffordshire.

* * *

How long T C stayed at Beck, Wild & Co., is not recorded, or indeed where he subsequently worked during the next five years - apart from a brief spell at Taylor, Wain & Bates` factory in Longton. He (T C) later recounted that in this period he tried various jobs, such as mould-making, turning and modelling.

In around 1878 he signed up as an apprentice 'thrower' at Albert Barlow's factory, which was the 'Old Cyples`s Pottery' in Market Street, Longton (see photos); he was now about thirteen years old.

The 1881 facade to the 'Old Cyple's Pottery' (2003)

The date stone, Old Cyple's Pottery (2003)

Pottery 'throwing', which involved making pots by hand from a lump of clay on a potter's wheel, was one of the most skilful jobs on a pot-bank, and the apprenticeship could take three or four years before the trainee became fully qualified.

T C must have learned quickly, and must also have impressed his masters, because in 1882, shortly before his eighteenth birthday, he was promoted to under-manager of the making shop.

But work was not the only thing on T C's mind. Being eighteen, and having the appetites of an eighteen year old, it was not long before his thoughts turned to the opposite sex.

A young girl from Longton caught his eye; she was Miss Emily Trickett, the only daughter of Edwin and Emma Trickett, family butchers in Cromartie Street, and although she was four years older than he, they were soon smitten with each other, and began 'courting'.

Things were going well now for T C. He was making great progress at work - he had his sights on another promotion - and, as he had found his soul-mate in Emily, and his job prospects looked good, the next logical step was marriage. So, in the summer of 1884 they 'tied the knot'.

* * *

It was seven o'clock on a Monday morning just a few weeks after he was married, that T C arrived for work as usual at the entrance to Barlow's factory. But what greeted him there this particular morning really took the wind out of his sails - the gates were locked and chained. *The works had closed down* (it was not unusual for pottery companies to close down without any warning).

T C was stunned - there had been no hint of any problems when he had finished work on the previous Saturday - and now here he was, standing on the pavement outside the factory, with no job and no prospects (and of course, no social security to turn to). He turned around and headed back home to break the news to his unsuspecting wife.

Although a blow like this would have overwhelmed a lot of men, T C was made of sterner stuff. The next day he was out in Longton looking for work - and he found it - starting work at 'Jones and Howson' as a thrower that same day.

But this episode had had a salutary effect on T C; no more would he rely on just one source of income, diversification was the key to a worry-free future, he reasoned - and this was the path that he trod for the rest of his life - with remarkable results.

* * *

T C worked hard in his new job; often being one of the first to arrive in the morning, and the last to leave at night. He volunteered for any overtime that was going, and could even be found at his bench all through the week-end, if there were orders to complete.

He saved his money diligently, and within a couple of years, had enough put by to invest in a small grocer's shop in Stafford Street (The Strand). His wife Emily ran the shop, whilst T C continued as a thrower at the factory.

T C had bought wisely - the shop did well, so well in fact that it was not long before another grocer's shop was purchased, No. 26 Commerce Street - adjoining the new Empire Theatre. And very soon after, yet another shop, this time No. 187 High Street (Uttoxeter Road), a confectionery and fruit shop.

187 High Street (2003)

At about this time, just down from the High Street shop, on the opposite side of the road, T C`s elder brother, Holland Leese Wild, was running a public house, the 'Dog and Partridge'

The Dog & Partridge (2003)

In about 1890, T C, who was by now becoming quite comfortably off, invested a little of his money into a small pot-bank in Clayton Street, Longton, although, as a silent partner he had no say in the running of the business.
At about the same time, his father, who had earlier relinquished his share of the pottery in Anchor Road, now became a junior partner in the firm of *'Dresden Porcelain Co.'*, in the High Street, Longton (This was one of the companies being run by the up-and-coming Thomas

Forester, of the Phoenix Works - see *'A Victorian Pottery - Thos. Foresters`*, No 1 in this series)

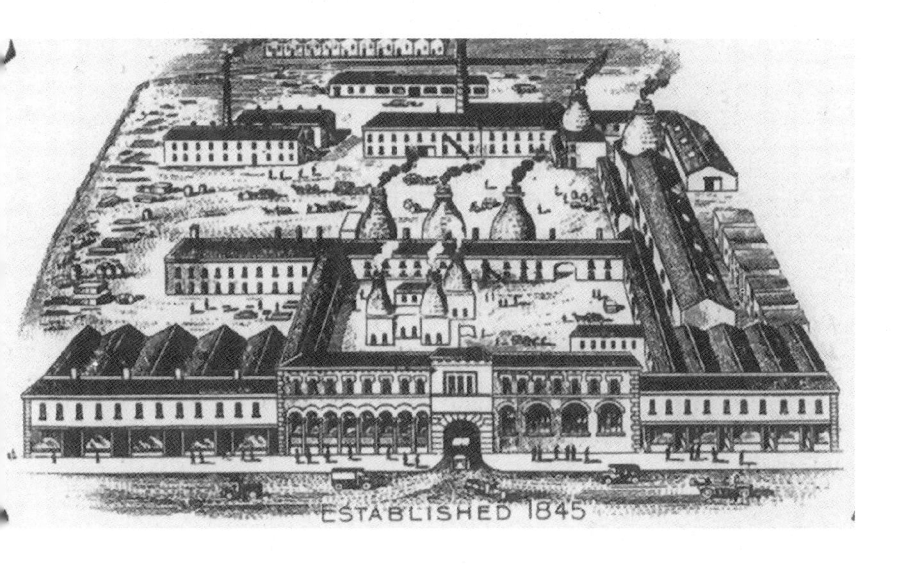

A Drawing of the Dresden Porcelain Co, High Street, c1910

In September 1894, T C celebrated his thirtieth birthday. He was now the owner of three successful shops in the town, had a share in a small pot-bank, and was still working as a thrower.

With all the various jobs he had tried, and the different firms he had worked for, he had gained a great deal of knowledge and experience of the potting trade, and, coupled with a not inconsiderable amount of finance available (albeit, most of it tied up), he was in a good position to take advantage of the favourable situation that was to come his way early in the new year.

Chapter Two

Getting Down To Business

Early in 1895, Thomas Wild Snr. approached his son T C, with a proposition. He had heard that the old 'Albert Works' in the High Street (Uttoxeter Road), Longton, was up for sale at a very good price, and he suggested that they might buy it between them, and run it as a china manufactory in *their name*.

This was just what T C had been waiting for. He immediately sold his share of the Clayton Street business and his shop in Stafford Street to raise the necessary capital. Within six months, he was in business with his father, running the firm of 'Thomas Wild & Co., at the Albert Works, High Street, Longton.

Albert Works:
Situated on the north side of High Street (Uttoxeter Road), between Lower Hill Street (Landon Street) and Middle Hill Street (Harber Street), it was built around 1846, and was named after Queen Victoria's Consort, Prince Albert.
James Beech was the first owner of the then three oven china works, making inexpensive tea, breakfast and dessert wares. Around 1860, the trade style was changed to James Beech & Son, and they were reported as making *'more than ordinary china tea ware'*.

After the death of James Beech and his son in the 1880s, the works passed to Mr Stephen Mear, but the firm continued to trade, however, under the old name.

It appears that there were several short term owners after this date, and the works began to get a bit run down (hence the 'good price').

In 1895 it was acquired by Thomas Wild and Thomas Clarke Wild.

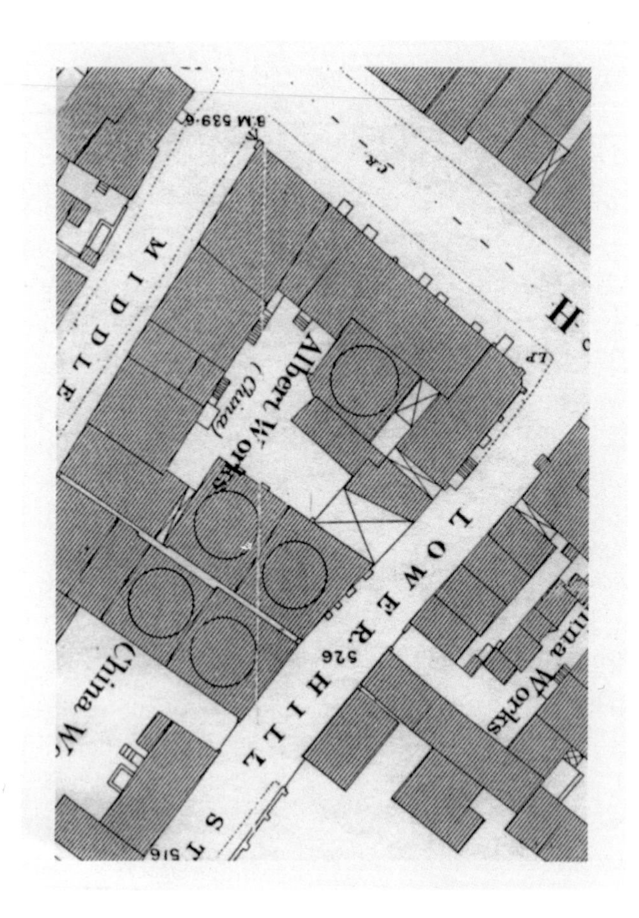

O S Map of The Albert Works, 1878 (High St. Running from the top centre to middle right)

Right from the outset, the Wilds were determined to produce only 'useful wares' at the Albert Works - by this they meant only items that could be used at the dining-room table. There would be no vases made, or figurines, or anything else that one could not eat of drink from. Tea, breakfast and dessert ware was the order of the day for this new company, and both Thomas Senior and Thomas Junior realised that these were the articles of bone china that were most in demand by the buying public. They would let companies such as Thomas Foresters`, Sampson Smiths` and The Royal Art Pottery make all the other 'fancy' stuff.

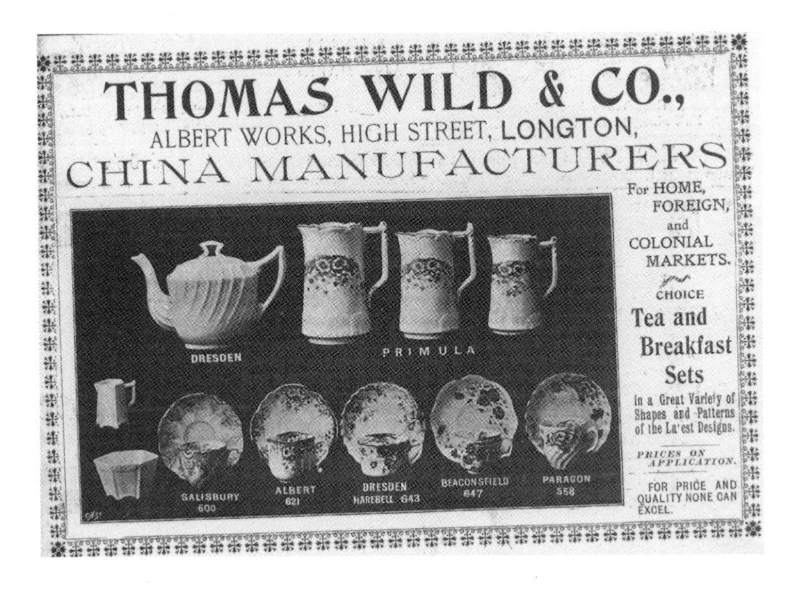

Advertisment from the *Pottery Gazette*, 1897

Most of Longton`s pottery manufacturers at this time were making china ware exclusively (in 1897, there were over sixty different china companies operating in the town), so, for a small inexperienced china manufacturer such as Thomas Wild & Co., to survive, they must be capable of either producing goods that were cheaper than the competition, or, of a better quality than the rest, yet still remain competitive on price.

This was where T C`s experience of working for a number of china producers proved invaluable. He had worked for both ends of the trade - the cheap and cheerful (Beck, Wild & Co., etc) and the relatively better class of producers such as Barlow's, so he had seen at close hand how both factions operated.

With the agreement of his father he set out to make only good quality wares, but at an economical price. This, he reasoned, meant using three main criteria: a) limiting the variety of shapes made (longer runs of one product are more cost effective); b) choosing a better class of decoration, but ones which were also easy to apply; and c) only employing workers who were prepared to perform their jobs properly and carefully - *but not necessarily for any higher pay* (this involved quite a lot of hiring and firing until the required standard of worker was reached - but this was one area of management that never troubled T C, or his successors).

* * *

English bone china has a number of attributes that set it apart from other types of porcelain. It is, of course, translucent - hold it up to the light, and one can see the outline of one's fingers through the ware. It is also of a very pleasant shade of white; not a bluey white as is a lot of continental porcelain, nor is it a grey white like most oriental china, but is a soft, subtle, almost pearly white. And it is also capable of being very finely potted; in other words, the tea-cups, saucers or whatever can be made very thin and lightweight - a feature much approved of by the tea-party hostesses of the nineteenth and early twentieth century.

It was probably T C`s insistence on a 'fineness of potting' that gained the factory a lot of repeat orders. In an article in the *'Pottery Gazette'* of 1898, the travelling reporter, examining Wild`s wares, commented *"....the tea-cups are particularly fine-lipped, a feature much loved by the ladies"*.

T. Wild's wares of 1898

1897 saw the Diamond Jubilee of Queen Victoria - the sixty years of her rule had seen Britain, and the British way of life change for ever, in so many ways.

There were celebrations by her subjects in every city, town and village in the land, and Thomas Wild Snr. paid his own small tribute by composing some verses in her honour, and sending them to the Queen personally.

"Lines on the Record reign.

All hail the record reign,
Of Britain's noblest Queen;
Who in ruling her subjects in love,
Found equal time to serve her God.

And having ruled with power,
Her great and vast domain;
In giving freedom to her slaves,
In honour of God's name.

Her shield and buckler is her God,
Her subjects are her joy;
A nobler life than hers has not,
Been lived by Queen before.

Then raise the joyful strain,
To earths remotest bound;
The diamond Jubilee is come,
With one accord rejoice around.

And when her race is run,
A tribute we must raise;
Unto her noble heart,
A monument of praise.

Then let us all with merry bliss,
Note well her life serene;
And may she by her actions gain,
Eternal life supreme."

T Wild, Belgrave Road, Florence.

In reply, Thomas received a letter on July 6th from Buckingham Palace, in which the Queen's Private Secretary said he had been commanded by Her Majesty to thank Mr Thomas Wild for his letter of the 28th June, and for the accompanying verses.

* * *

But Thomas Snr. was not in good health. He had been ill for quite a while, and in the summer of 1898 he died, aged just fifty seven. This left T C as the sole proprietor of the Albert Works - a fact he was not slow to publicise (see the advertisement for 1899).

Advertisement from the *Pottery Gazette*, 1899

* * *

The pottery industry by its very diverse nature (delicate, nimble processes such as decorating and gilding alongside heavy, manual work such as clay preparation and oven firing), has always meant that there would be as many women as men working on the shop-floor - and very often working in close proximity to each other (a fact which would have led to many ‘involvements’ - some of which might have led to marriage - *and probably just as many that led to divorce*).

But although the ratio of women to men in the pottery factories was roughly fifty-fifty, in common with all women at this time, women were generally regarded as second class citizens - even in such basic areas as terms of employment.

On the 6th of July 1899, at the Longton County Court, Sarah Allen of Longton, a scourer working at T Wild & Co., sued her employer for £2 5s (£2 25p), being £2 for wrongful dismissal, and 5s (25p) in respect of a deduction from the plaintiff's wages.

Sarah Allen's case was that she was in charge of the scouring shop. On May 13th her employer gave her a week's notice, whereas she was entitled to more.

His Honour Judge Jordan, in his summing up, said that all through the potting trade a month's notice was the rule - he had seventeen years experience, and had never found anything different, so therefore he found for the plaintiff.

In the August edition of the *'Pottery Gazette'* the editor, referring to the above case, stated indignantly *"....although Judge Jordan may have had seventeen years experience in the potting trade, any potter could tell his Honour that with WOMEN, a WEEK`S notice was the rule, and was so every day that passed"*.

* * *

On New Year's Day 1900, upwards of a hundred employees and staff of the Albert Works met at the Dunrobin Hotel, Stone Road (Lightwood Road), for a dinner given to honour their employer, Mr Thomas Clarke Wild.

An illuminated address and portraits of T C and his wife were presented by Mr Lester, the oldest workman of the firm.

Mr Wild thanked them all for the cordiality with which they had received him, and for the 'interesting and tangible expression of their esteem represented by the portraits'

Who paid for this gathering at the Dunrobin is not recorded - it would certainly not have been the workpeople (not with the wages they were being paid!). It is more than likely that this was a public relations exercise, engineered and paid for by T C himself.

As the new century unfolded, Thomas Clarke Wild was making quite a name for himself as a businessman of some note.

In 1903 he was made a director of the Longton Mutual Permanent Building Society (becoming president in 1917); he was also Church Warden of Normacot, and at the Albert Works, he was in the enviable position of having more orders for his tea and breakfast ware than he could fulfil (the style of the company had by now changed to *'Thos. C Wild'*).

Advertisement from the *Pottery Gazette*, 1904

In June 1905, T C`s eldest son, Master T E Wild (known as Tom) began his career at the Albert Works. He was just short of his fifteenth birthday and was put to work in the 'clay-end' (pot-banks - although the different departments were usually jumbled together in no logistical order - have always been metaphorically divided into two separate 'ends': the 'clay-end' which covers all the processes that deal with the wares in their clay state, i.e., before they are fired in the ovens, and the 'decorating-end', which more or less speaks for itself).

Master Tom was told that he would have to serve a five year apprenticeship, working his way through all the various departments of the factory until he was fully conversant with every aspect of china production, when he would then join the management team.

Later that same year, 1905, T C realised one of his many dreams. It was thus:

A few years earlier, when he was running the fruit shop in the High Street, T C would very often stand in the shop doorway gazing across at the frontage of the 'St Mary's Works' - a well built pot-bank being run by the Moore Bros - which stood directly opposite the shop.

"One day" he would say repeatedly to his wife *"I will own that factory"*.

In the autumn of 1905, he realised this ambition when the owner, the world famous ceramist, Mr Bernard Moore, left the firm to become a consultant potter in Wolfe Street (Kingsway), Stoke, and put the works up for sale. T C purchased the property immediately.

St Mary's Works (2003)

Date stone on the front of St. Mary's Works

St Mary's Works:

The original St Mary's Works were built by Samuel Moore in 1862 (still standing today, 2003).

Samuel Moore had started potting in 1840 as one half of the partnership of *'Hamilton & Moore'*, in a small pot-bank on the opposite side of High Street. Here they made the crude, poorly finished china that so many of the factories of Longton were turning out at the time. In the *'Pottery Examiner'* of September 1846, they were referred to as being amongst *'the spoil trade employers who sold cheaply and paid badly'*.

Hamilton left the partnership in 1859, and in 1862 Samuel Moore built the St Mary's Works, where he continued on his own until his son Bernard joined him in 1867 when the firm became *'Moore & Son'*

Bernard Moore

Five years later, Samuel retired, and Bernard was joined by his brother Samuel Vincent Moore - the company was now known as *'Moore Bros'*, and was responsible for making some very high quality, highly decorative china.

In the 1880s, an elaborate, typically Victorian extension was built on to the frontage of the works, and in 1905 T C Wild purchased the buildings, complete with fixtures and fittings.

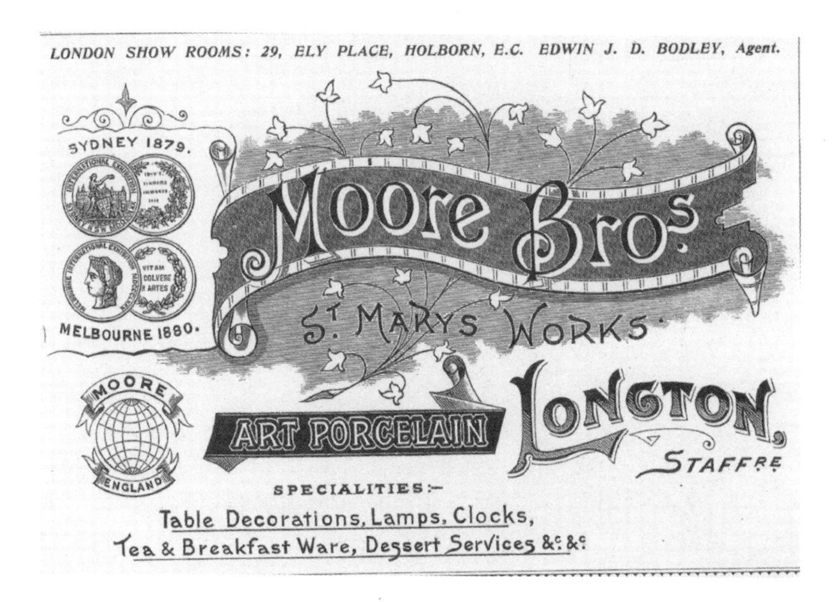

Advertisement for *'Moore Bros.'*

Initially, T C used the St Mary's Works for decorating purposes only - the white ware being transported the 500 yards or so from the Albert Works by horse and cart (no doubt with many breakages).

As the new works was gradually equipped and furnished to T C`s satisfaction, so more and more of the *'Royal Albert Crown China'* was manufactured on site, until eventually almost all the china was being made in what was to become T C Wild`s flagship works.

* * *

It was during these first years at the St Mary's Works that T C began making his famous 'Longton Derby' china. This was a direct copy of a well-known design being produced by the celebrated firm of 'Royal Crown Derby'.

T C`s design was first printed in under-glaze claret brown, then panelled in mazarine blue, enamelled in red and illuminated with bright gold.

Although it was not as expertly decorated, and the body was not as perfect as that of Royal Crown Derby, it was nevertheless very attractive, and was *considerably cheaper* than the original. It sold in vast quantities and was probably the biggest selling line in bone china the trade had ever seen. T C became known far and wide as 'The Derby King'.

In 1907, T C`s second son Fred joined the company, and like his brother Tom, was put to work on the shop-floor and told to acquire experience of every process of china production.

Meanwhile, T C had branched out yet again, this time he had gone into partnership with his brother James Shelley Wild to take over the pottery concern of *'Adderley and Lawson'* at the 'Salisbury Works' and the 'Crown China Works', both in Edensor Road, Longton. They renamed the firm *'Wild Bros'*, where they made china tea -ware for the cheaper end of the market.

By the end of the first decade of the twentieth century, T C had become a very busy man. He was now running four pot-banks: the Albert Works, St Mary's Works, Salisbury Works and the Crown China Works. He was also looking after his business interests in the Longton Permanent Mutual Building Society and tending to his work for the Church at Normacot.

But this was just a small part of what was to come in the following twenty years.

Chapter Three

Onwards and Upwards

On the 31st of March 1910, the separate towns that formed 'The Potteries' - Tunstall, Burslem, Hanley, Stoke-upon-Trent, Fenton and Longton - became unified under the name of the *County Borough of Stoke-on-Trent*. The six communities ceased to have separate existence, and their Councils were dissolved. Federation had arrived after many, many years of negotiation. The number of Councillors for the new Borough was to be 78 with 26 Aldermen, a total of 104. The first election of Councillors, three for each of the 26 wards, was held on March 22nd, and the new Council met for the first time on March 31st at the North Stafford Hotel, Stoke. Thomas Clarke Wild was later elected as Councillor for Ward 26.

Later that same year, T C purchased the ***'Park Place Works'*** (still standing, 2003) in the High Street almost opposite the Albert Works. These works - part of which date back to the 1770s when the land was owned by the Shelley Brothers - had been carried on as a china manufactory by *'Rowley & Newton'* from 1895 until they finally closed down in 1905, since when the factory had remained empty.

In a statement made at the time, T C said that the works would re-open as a china factory as soon as the necessary alterations had been made.

The Park Place Works (2003)

It was around this time that Master Tom was coming to the end of his 'apprenticeship' - he had spent time learning all he could in the various departments of the St Mary's Works, and was now deemed to be fully conversant with every aspect of bone china production.

It had previously been arranged by T C that as soon as Tom reached the age of twenty, he was to go into the 'sales' side of management, and this had (reluctantly) been agreed by Tom himself.

But Tom was happier down in the 'clay-end' of the factory, where he was often to be found whenever he had a spare moment - much to the chagrin of his father, who had repeatedly forbidden him to go there.

It all came to a head one day, when yet again Tom had gone missing, and this time T C, after searching high and low, confronted him in one of the casting-shops.

Not a word was said, nor did one need to be said, as a red-faced Tom scurried out of the work-shop like a scalded cat, leaving a rather flustered T C to force an embarrassed smile for the benefit of the astonished casters (it would not do for the 'workers' to see the management falling out between themselves).

Nothing else was said for the rest of the day, but as T C was driving himself and his two sons home in the pony and trap that evening, he suddenly stopped the trap, and grasping the arm of young Tom with one hand and holding the riding whip up aloft with the other, said, *"If I catch you down the clay-end once more Tom, I'll use this whip on you"*.

He released Tom's arm, started the pony, and completed the rest of the journey in silence. Tom never went down the clay-end again without permission.

* * *

On October 12th, T C`s eldest daughter, Emily Francis, married Mr James Hereward Poole in the little village church at Normacot. Mr Poole was the grandson of Thomas Poole of the Cobden Works, Cooke Street, Longton, founder of the famous 'Royal Stafford China`.

Normacot Church (2003)

The following year, 1911, saw the Park Place Works reopen as a china manufactory, making white ware only, principally for the colonial market. A Mr Harry Reid - who for the past fourteen years had been the travelling representative for T C`s Royal Albert Crown China - was installed as manager of the works. As with all of T C`s factories, the Park Place Works had been thoroughly modernised with all the latest labour-saving machinery - to give *maximum* profitability.

Warren Street, a typical Longton scene.

June 14th saw T C`s second daughter, Ethel, marry Mr Wilfred Beswick, fifth son of Mr James Wright Beswick of Belgrave House, Trentham Road, Longton. The bridegroom's father, Mr J W Beswick was the owner of the famous earthenware manufacturer *'John Beswick'* of Gold Street, Longton.

Again the service was held at Normacot`s little church, but because T C had recently been quite ill, and was now convalescing, Miss Ethel was given away by her brother Tom.

After the wedding party had partaken of the wedding breakfast at Lightwood House (T C`s residence - since demolished and replaced by what is now, 2003, the 'Lightwood Tavern'), Mr and Mrs Beswick departed for their honeymoon in North Wales.

Trentham Road with the 'Lord John Russell' on the corner, Beswick's house was few yards further up.

The St Mary's Works was now, as stated earlier, the main factory and head offices for *'Thos C Wild'*. The Albert Works was still making white ware for decoration at the St Mary's Works, and the Park Place Works was making predominately plain white tea and dessert ware. But, as the public's demand for decorated ware became irresistible, T C rang the changes.

The Park Place Works was the first to change, when, in 1913, T C invited Harry Reid, the manager of the works, to buy a half share of the factory. Reid jumped at this opportunity, and so subsequently became a fellow director (along with T C) of the new company, Reid & Co., of the Park Place Works. He immediately set about developing a brand image for his own, medium class, tea and dessert ware (although, as would always be the case, T C was on hand to see that standards did not fall).

Harry Reid

The Albert Works was the next to be reorganized, when, a little while later, a William Thomas Chapman (the son of the proprietor of the old established firm of 'Chapman`s') of Shooter's Hills, Longton, joined T C on the board of directors of a new company called *'Chapman`s (Longton) Ltd.*, of the Albert Works, Longton.

William Chapman

Will Chapman was installed as managing director of the new company, and wasted no time in setting his stall out as to what the firm would be producing. He had noticed that certain continental productions were now no longer available in the UK - these were the white 'china' specialities such as flower-tubes, fern pots, small candle-sticks etc., which had been formerly manufactured in Austria, and usually made of opaque earthenware, glazed to resemble bone china.

Chapman reasoned that this was a niche in the market that he could profitably exploit, and, with the help of T C, set about making quality *'bone china'* items, at a competitive price (see advertisement).

All ware produced at the Albert Works from now on would be identified and stamped as *'Standard China'*.

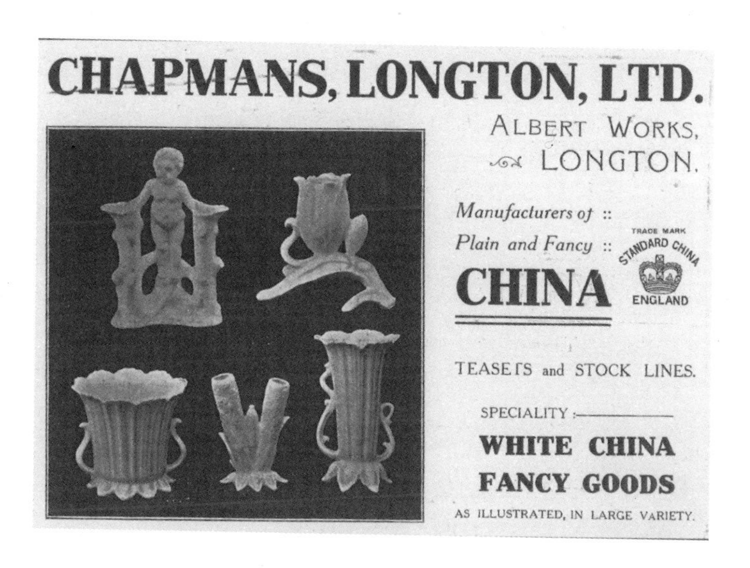

Advertisement for Chapman's, Longton, Ltd.

At the end of February 1913, T C`s wife Emily, died - she was 53, and had been in poor health for a while. They had been married for 29 years, and she had borne him eleven children: nine daughters and two sons, all of which survived.

T C was heartbroken, and immediately threw himself into his work in an effort to lessen the pain. But what he really needed, he soon realised, was something new to occupy his mind - and it wasn't long before a novel idea occurred to him.

He had become aware of a new phenomenon that was sweeping the country - *the moving picture show* (he had recently viewed a showing of this new medium at the Empire Theatre in Longton) and the idea came to him that the good people of Normacot deserved a 'Picture Palace' of their very own, and that he was the man to build them one!

So, very shortly afterwards he purchased a plot of land in Upper Normacot Road (not far from Victoria Road, where he had lived as a child) for that very purpose, and early in the new year (1914), arranged for the building of a new 'picture-palace' - which was to be called ***'The Alhambra'***.

After the official opening later that year, T C, although the sole proprietor, left the running of the cinema to the new manager, Mr Henry Baskeyfield.

Although the Alhambra was not the first establishment in the Potteries to show the new 'moving-pictures', it was the first building in the area to be built *solely* for that purpose (the others being former theatres or music halls which had been converted).

Mr Baskeyfield remained the manager until the early nineteen twenties when a Mr Leveson - Myatt took over, later to be joined by his brother Arthur (who, together, purchased the Alhambra from the

Wild family in 1945, and ran it very successfully, until it finally closed down in 1977).

The Alhambra Picture Palace

T C now found himself a victim of his own success, for although he was by now quite a wealthy man, he was also a very busy one. So busy was he now with his many pot-banks, his directorship of the building society, his duties as a Councillor and his work for the church that he found he had little time left over to spend with his beloved children, whom he feared, might become neglected.

But, as always seemed to happen throughout T C`s life, whenever a problem reared its head, a solution was never very far away, and this time the solution was a very pleasant one.

On January 6th 1915, he married for the second time. His new bride was Miss Ada Eaves, the eldest daughter of Thomas Eaves of The Hawthorns, King's Heath, Birmingham. The bride's father was a well known clock and clock-case maker.

As with his first wife, T C had again chosen well - Ada Wild went on to provide him with a loving and stable home for his children, whilst he busied himself building his empire.

Ada Wild

In 1917 the Wild family moved into Blythe House, a large mansion standing at the side of the main road running through Blythe Bridge - a little village on the outskirts of the Potteries. Blythe House had, in the past, been the residence of various dignitaries from the Potteries, men such as the infamous Charles Harvey, proprietor of Harvey's Bank in Longton (whose business dealings in the 1860s, caused many firms to go bankrupt), and Alderman Bennion, former proprietor of the Crown and Anchor Hotel in Longton and several times mayor of Longton. The Wild family were to spend many happy years in this beautiful house, with its own tennis courts, and rambling orchard.

Later that year, T C took his sons into the company, which was now designated, *'Thos. C Wild & Sons.*

Blythe House (Blythe Bridge High School now stands on this site)

In January the following year, William Coggins of 33 Ricardo Street, Dresden, died. Mr Coggins had been the junior partner in the firm of *'Shore & Coggins'* (originally Shore Coggins & Holt) at the Edensor Works, New Street (now Greendock Street), Longton.

Shore & Coggins was a medium size concern making cheap and rather poorly made tea-ware

Ricardo Street. Coggins lived half way along the street, on the left.

A few weeks later, the remaining partner, John Shore, of 67 Cromartie Street, Longton, decided that at 71 years of age, it was time to retire, and subsequently put the works up for sale as a going concern.

T C immediately purchased the complete business - then proceeded to close down the factory whilst he made the necessary alterations needed, to facilitate the making of a better class of goods at a more competitive price.

An early drawing of the Edensor Works.

Within twelve months the 'new' factory was ready to begin production. In a later edition of the 'Pottery Gazette', their correspondent, on viewing the refurbished factory, wrote,

"*....few factories in Longton have been so virtually turned inside out within so short a space of time in order to render possible a vast improvement of the finished product and a real expansion of the business generally. Certain it is that there is no factory in Longton today whose internal arrangements are cleaner or more up-to-date in every detail. Hand power, in practically every department, has given place to motive power, and from the sliphouse upwards there is apparent everywhere a smoothness and easiness of working that is a marked change from the rather cumbersome old types of appliances that were formally in operation at the self-same factory.*

"As to the finished productions, these reflect the wonderful changes that have taken place in regard to the factory equipment."

At about the same time that the Edensor Works were undergoing their transformation, T C purchased another well-known and well-respected china factory - William Lowe's Sydney Works in Sutherland Road, Longton.

William Lowe had originally gone into the potting business in 1865 with a John Tams as *'Tams & Lowe'* operating from the St. Gregory's Works, High Street, Longton (situated on the eastern corner of Wharf Street and Uttoxeter Road).

These works, built around 1794 were in a very poor condition when this partnership started production (earthenware only). Shortly afterwards, at Lowe's instigation, they began to introduce bone china (although in a very limited way to begin with).

William Lowe

In 1875, John Tams left the company to start his own business (the famous *'John Tams Ltd'*, of the Crown Works, Longton - still going strong today, 2004) leaving Lowe as the sole proprietor. In 1879 he built the Sydney Works in Sutherland Road, to the rear of the St. Gregory's Works, for the exclusive production of bone china - gradually phasing out the making of earthenware at the old factory.

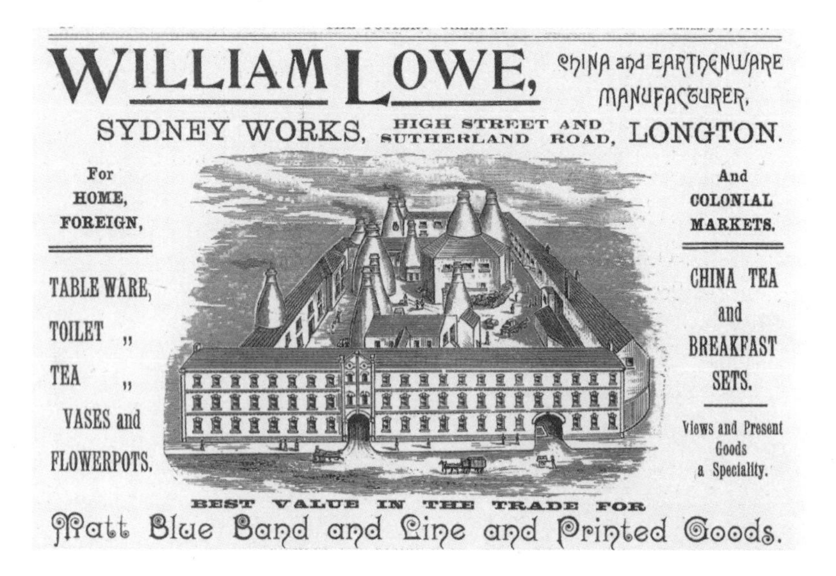

Advertisement for *William Lowe*

At the Longton Borough Police Courts in October 1883, a Mr Edward Eardley appeared charged with the embezzlement of various sums of money belonging to Mr William Lowe, manufacturer, Sydney Works, Longton.

Mr Eardley had been engaged as a commercial traveller, at a salary, for William Lowe, but owing to his conduct not being satisfactory, was taken off salary and given one more chance, this time on a commission only basis. The terms being 7 per cent, with 3 per cent to go towards the arrears of previous journeys.

Before he set out, Eardley told his employer that he had no money, so Mr Lowe advanced him a sum of £5 towards his expenses It was arranged that Eardley should travel around Lancashire only, which he appeared to have done, and according to his book, collected £118 13s 6d, of which he sent home only £96 13s 6d, leaving a shortfall of £22 not accounted for.

Eardley should then have returned to the factory, but instead of doing so, he appeared to have visited several towns outside the district assigned to him, where he collected a further £26 16s, which, with the £22, and the £5 advance meant he had a total of £51 16s belonging to his employer.

Eardley then went to Liverpool and took a ticket for the United States.

Unfortunately for him he appeared to have had a very strong likeness to the manager of the Union Bank of Birmingham, who had absconded, and this led to his arrest by the police at Liverpool who believed that they had caught their man. On being searched, papers were found on his possession showing he came from Longton. Enquiries were made at the Sydney Works and Eardley was arrested, charged with embezzlement, and later brought back to Longton to stand trial.

* * *

William Lowe died on March 13th 1898, and the factory continued more or less as before under the guidance of his executors, until purchased by Thomas Clarke Wild.

An early drawing of the Sydney Works

The Sydney Works today (2004)

Date stone, Sydney Works

A few days before Christmas 1918, T C organised a Christmas dinner at the Town Hall, Longton. Over a thousand workers who were employed at the various factories of which T C had interests were present.

In the foreword to the souvenir programme, it said *"A bond of comradeship and sympathy happily exists amongst us, which is most gratifying to those whose duty it is to guide this policy and manage the affairs of our various businesses"*. And again *"So long as we all work together harmoniously, and with the same spirit of mutual respect and goodwill, we may look forward with great confidence to the future, which it is hoped may be filled with health, happiness and prosperity for our employees and their families"*.

The trade papers at the time made a great deal of this *'generous and sincere token of respect'* by an employer to his workers (and they may well have been sincere in their thinking), but, in hindsight, knowing now what poor wages the pottery industry paid at this time, together with the punishing work-load that the workers were forced to accept - or suffer the consequences - it is hard, today, to bestow very much respect onto the shoulders of any of these employers (although T C was perhaps not as tyrannical as some manufacturers at this time, neither was he particularly known for his benevolence).

Typical worker's cottages
Short Street, Longton, 2003. Little changed from a hundred years ago.

Chapter Four

The Works

The beginning of the nineteen twenties saw T C as possibly the leading industrialist in Stoke-on-Trent, and without question one of the busiest manufacturers in North Staffordshire.

It might be useful at this juncture, to give a brief résumé of all the pottery manufacturing businesses in which T C had an interest.
They were:

T C Wild & Sons. St Mary's Works, High Street, Longton. Royal Albert China

Chapman`s. Albert Works, High Street, Longton. Standard China

Reid & Co. Park Place Works, High Street, Longton. Roslyn China.

Shore & Coggins. Edensor Works, New Street, Longton. Bell China.

William Lowe. Sydney Works, Sutherland Road, Longton. Court China.

Wild & Adams. Royal Crown Pottery, Warren Street, Longton. Earthenware.

Blair's (Longton) Ltd. Beaconsfield Pottery, Anchor Road, Longton. China

Barlow's (Longton) Ltd. Melbourne Works, Church Street, Longton. Earthenware.

T W Barlow & Son Ltd. Coronation Works, Commerce Street, Longton. Earthenware.

Thomas Cone Alma Works High Street, Longton. Earthenware.

Colclough & Co Stanley Works, Stafford Street, Longton. Royal Stanley Earthenware.

Burgess Bros. Carlisle Works, High Street, Longton. Earthenware.

There was also the firm of 'Wild Bros.' in Edensor Road, Longton, which, as stated earlier, was owned by T C and his brother James Shelley Wild. In 1922 T C relinquished his share of the concern, leaving his brother as the sole proprietor.

In 1923 Thomas Clarke Wild was made a Justice of the Peace for Longton.

Two years later, at the end of a Royal visit to Burslem by their Majesties, King George V and Queen Mary, the King took everyone by surprise when he announced that the status of the Borough of Stoke-on-Trent was henceforward to be raised to that of a *city*.

It was perhaps in recognition of the growing importance of the Potteries as a major manufacturing area, that the old Borough was now to be known as the **'City of Stoke-on-Trent'**.

King George V and Queen Mary

Royal Albert

CROWN CHINA

WE EXTEND A
HEARTY INVITATION
to all Buyers to visit our Works when in the Potteries, or if more convenient see our Samples at our London Showrooms:
G. A. DUBERY & CO., 24, THAVIES INN, E.C.1.

Thomas C. Wild & Sons.

St. Mary's China Works,
Longton, Stoke-on-Trent.

Advertisement from the *Pottery Gazette*, 1925

Advertisement from the *Pottery Gazette*, 1907

Early Drawing of the Alma Works (*Thos. Cone*)

Early Drawing of the Melbourne Works *Barlow's (Longton) Ltd*

SHORE & COGGINS.

Edensor Works, LONGTON, Stoke-on-Trent.

Telephone: LONGTON 482.

CHINA MANUFACTURERS.

SPECIALITIES—China Tea and Breakfast Sets.

General Stock lines, etc.

BADGED WARE FOR HOTELS, RESTAURANTS, Etc.

Illustrated Sheets and Price Lists on application.

New Zealand Representative:
J. D. ROBERTS, LTD.,
49, Customs Street East,
Auckland,
New Zealand.

South Africa:
A. E. HARRIS,
126, Market Street,
P.O. Box 1199,
Johannesburg,
South Africa.

Australia:
HAYNES & CO.,
Kensington,
Sydney,
N.S.W.

Advertisement from the *'Pottery Gazette'* 1922

REID & CO.,

— Park Place China Works, —
High St., LONGTON, STOKE-ON-TRENT.

Telephone: LONGTON 168.

CHINA MANUFACTURERS

FOR HOME AND EXPORT SPECIALITIES.

CHINA TEA & BREAKFAST SETS.

GENERAL STOCK LINES, Etc.

BADGED WARE FOR HOTELS, RESTAURANTS, Etc.

ILLUSTRATED SHEETS & PRICE LISTS ON APPLICATION.

New Zealand Representative:
J. E. SUTCLIFFE,
Central Sample Rooms, Court House Lane,
Auckland, New Zealand.

South African Representative:
EDWIN WILSON & CO.,
Box 719, 144, Longmarket Street,
Cape Town, South Africa.

Australian Representative:
J. BARTLETT BROWNE & CO.,
Daking House, Rawson Place,
Sydney, Australia.

LONDON AGENT - - -

A. R. MARSHALL & CO., Gamage Buildings, 118/122, HOLBORN, E.C.1.

Advertisement from the *'Pottery Gazette'* 1922

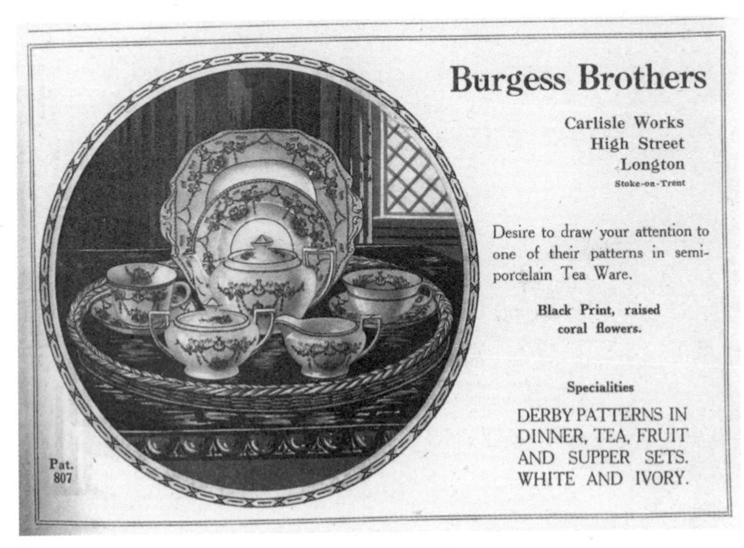

Advertisement from the *'Pottery Gazette'* 1930

Shore and Coggins, Edensor Works in the 1940s

Placing an oven at Shore & Coggins

Setting an enamel kiln at Shore & Coggins

Cup-handlers, Shore & Coggins

'The quality shines through'
An advertisement from the *'Pottery Gazette & Glass Trade Review'*, 1951

Chapter Five

Chief Citizen

On the 1st of June 1927, T C`s younger brother James Shelley Wild, of 'The Beeches', Meir, Stoke-on-Trent died. He had been ill for some months, and had recently gone into a Manchester nursing home in order that an operation might be performed, two days after which, he passed away.

He had been a keen golfer and bowler, being a member of the Meir Golf Club, and the Florence Bowling Club.

The works, the Salisbury and Crown China Works, of which he was the sole proprietor, were sold to a Leslie H Bradley, who began producing *'Salisbury China'* almost immediately. (Salisbury China was eventually taken over by Thomas Poole of the Cobden Works in1961).

In November of the same year, T C received some good news - very good news in fact. He was to become the first Mayor of the 'new' City of Stoke-on-Trent - its first **'chief citizen'**.

In the summer of the following year, 1928, the news got even better when His Majesty the King gave the royal assent, on July 10th, for the chief Magistrate of Stoke-on-Trent to bear in future, the title of 'Lord Mayor' - T C becoming one of only seventeen Lord Mayors in the whole of England and Wales.

T C Wild, Lord Mayor

Thomas Clarke Wild had finally made it! He had risen from the humblest of beginnings (jigger-turner in a run-down factory at the age of eight and a half) to the highest office in the city.

In a report in the *'Pottery Gazette and Glass Trade Review'* of August 1928, it said, amongst the many eulogies:

"Mr Wild`s career is a standing testimony that hard work and ambition can lift the ordinary worker out of a common rut, providing he has initiative and opportunity".

And *"The satisfactory thing is that in no quarter is the present Lord Mayor of Stoke-on-Trent grudged the honour which his hard-working life has brought him in the fullness of his experience".*

As was always the case throughout his life, whenever TC took on a new venture, he would always put one hundred per cent effort into the task. And so it was with his new role as Lord Mayor - but by this time, circumstances had changed.

T C had found that being the chief citizen of such an important and expanding city as Stoke-on-Trent was no small undertaking, what with civic functions, public appearances, etc., all eating into his working day, there was not the time left to oversee the vast manufacturing empire that he had built up. He was also now sixty-four years of age, and despite still having the enthusiasm and hunger of a man half his age, there was no escaping the fact that he was slowing down.

So it was with a great deal of reluctance that T C prepared to hand over the reigns of all his pottery interests to his two sons, Tom and Fred.

* * *

As the two sons took more and more control over the business, so they began to do things their own way. One of the first things they did was to close down those factories which were either becoming uneconomical to sustain, or were duplicating the products of other, more successful factories.

`*Wild & Adams*` was the first to go - in fact T C had suspended production the previous year (1927), and, as the fabric of the factory was old and run-down, no more of the cheap earthenware was made there again.

1928 saw the sale of the `Stanley Pottery Ltd.,` of Edensor road, Longton. Always known as `*A Colclough & Co*`, the new owners were a Mr and Mrs Vernon of 33 Newport Street, Burslem.

Both of the above factories produced earthenware products only.

Two years later (1930) the Wilds closed two of their china factories:

William Lowe's Sydney Works in Sutherland Road, Longton, and *Blair's (Longton) Ltd.,* of the Beaconsfield Pottery, Anchor Road, Longton.

Although the Wilds were still major shareholders in the smaller concerns such as *Barlow's`, Thomas Cones`,* and *Burgess Bros* etc.,their investments, both in time and money now went into their four bigger companies; St. Mary's Works *(Royal Albert China)*, Park Place Works *(Roslyn China)*, Edensor Works (Shore & Coggins *Bell China*) and Albert Works (*Royal Standard China*).

An advertisement *Thos. Cone.*

T C, as was his wont, had, of course, being overseeing all of these operations, but most of his time during 1928 had been spent on his civic duties, and as with everything that T C had turned his hand to, he had made a complete success of his term in office.

* * *

In January 1929, a complementary dinner at Stoke Town Hall was held, the purpose of which was to give public expression for the services which T C had rendered to the city during his year in office.

It was a year in which he had conferred the freedom of the city upon three distinguished gentlemen - these were - Sir Oliver Lodge, the scientist from Penkhull, Stoke, who was the first to transmit a message by radio telegraphy, and who also invented the method of electrical spark ignition for the internal combustion engine (spark-plug); another was Stanley Baldwin (Prime Minister), and the third was Mr. Henry J Johnson, a ‘model employer and a generous contributor to charities’.

In answer to the many tributes that were paid to him during the course of the after-dinner speeches, T C thanked them all, and said that ‘he did not claim to be anything but a plain business man, but if he lacked anything as a public speaker he had certainly endeavoured to make up for this by his earnestness and sincerity’.

In the absence of Mrs. Wild due to illness, Miss Nora Wild, a daughter of the ex- Lord Mayor returned thanks, remarking that the past year had been one of the happiest of her life, and one that would live longest in her memory.

Advertisement for the ***new*** Singer Van, 1930

Towards the end of the year (1929) - a year which had seen T C praised by all for his sterling work as Lord Mayor, there appeared this report in *'The Pottery Gazette and Glass Trade Review'*, that praised another, much younger, son of Longton - but this time for a very different reason:

"LIFE LOST IN CROCKERY SEARCH - It is not often that one hears of a life being actually lost through searching for crockery, yet so remarkable and tragic an occurrence was brought to light in the Potteries recently. A Longton schoolboy of fourteen years of age, by name Richard J Sims, of Dresden, Longton, has been presented with the parchment of the Royal Humane Society in recognition of an attempt to save the life of a young man who, whilst searching a tip on the edge of a disused marl-hole, in order to find, if possible, some usable crockery in the shraff deposited there by a local firm of pottery manufacturers, fell into the water as a result of a fall of loose shraff. The boy Sims was an eye-witness of the occurrence, and seeing the man in difficulties, he dived into the water, which at one point is in the region of 100ft deep, and for a while held on to the man by his collar. In consequence, however, of the struggles of the man, the boy was compelled to release his hold and the man was drowned. In all the circumstances, and particularly in view of the fact that the sides of the marl-hole are steep and treacherous, this attempt at life-saving was rightly regarded as an act of real heroism, and it is pleasing to note that the Royal Humane Society has recognized it as such.

'Foxglove' Pattern

In November 1932, at the age of 68, T C finally retired. He had been playing less and less a role in the running of the business since his time as Lord Mayor, but now it was officially confirmed that he had severed his connection with the china trade completely, and that he was moving to his new residence: 'Rosslyn House', Russell Road, Rhyl, North Wales. His two sons, Tom and Fred would continue the business as before.

It is interesting to note that T C was just one of quite a number of pottery manufacturers, and pottery managers, who chose to spend the twilight of their years in this delightful sea-side town. And what with the yearly mass exodus of thousands of pottery workers, who habitually spent their summer holidays there in the first half of the twentieth century, Rhyl could almost have been called the 'Potteries by-the-sea'.

* * *

The following year saw T C Wild's become a Limited Company -

now to be known as 'T C Wild & Sons Ltd.', - with an initial Registered Capital of £15000 in £1 shares. The two permanent directors being; Mr. T E Wild of Park House, Longton, and Mr. F J Wild of Sutherland House, Blythe Bridge.

* * *

On December 13th 1937, Thomas Clarke Wild died peacefully in his sleep at his residence in Rhyl, North Wales. He was 73.

In his obituary in *'The Pottery Gazette & Glass Trade Review'*, as well as listing all the pottery factories in which T C had an interest (as chronicled earlier in this book), it also mentioned the many other activities of which he was involved in, and which gives some idea of the amazing energy and dynamism of the man.

Amongst these 'other activities', it said that he was: 'a Director and Vice-President of a prominent building society (Longton Permanent Mutual), Chairman of the Longton Cottage Hospital extension scheme, a School manager, a Justice of the Peace for the County, Chairman of Directors of the China and Earthenware Millers, Chairman and Proprietor of the Alhambra Picture House, a member of the Staffordshire Potteries Water Board, an Income Tax and Land Tax Commissioner, and a Freemason'.

The obituary went on to say:

"There are few men who can so stamp their mark upon an industry that the initials of their Christian names are alone sufficient to signalize their personality. Throughout the entire trade one needs only to hear the mention of the letters 'T C' to conjure up a virile personality, a keen business man and one of whom it has been well said that his triumph over early struggles was characteristic of his personal initiative and directional gifts.

Mr. T C Wild will assuredly be missed not only in the affairs of the china trade, but also by the social and administrative life of the Potteries."

The funeral took place at Normacot on December 19th.

T C left an estate worth £59,272 - a small fortune in 1937!

Market Street, Longton, at the turn of the century

Chapter Six

Expansion and Modernisation

Although by the late nineteen thirties the threat of war with Germany was gaining momentum, and the British people were becoming more and more uncertain as to their future, the two Wild brothers were concerning themselves more with the task of making the St. Mary's Works the most up-to-date china factory in the country.

Now that Tom and Fred had a clear field so to speak (without the giant shadow of TC hovering over them), they set about an expansion and modernisation programme at the St. Mary's Works, the like of which had not been seen before in Longton.

1937 saw the installation of an all-electric, continuous circular decorating kiln (see photo) which replaced a veritable battery of old-fashioned intermittently fired kilns (bottle ovens). This new kiln began operating on a three-shift system, seven days a week, and was capable of firing 8,000 dozens of decorated ware per week, *and with the minimum of labour.*

The new electric kiln

1939 saw the completion of a large, three-storey extension - 130ft in length and 30ft wide, the building of which involved digging and levelling the site before laying a reinforced concrete raft the whole length of the building.

Half of the top floor of this extension housed the new canteen, the other half, a modern casting-shop. The middle, or first floor, was for a biscuit scouring shop and warehouse, and also a new dipping-shop, whilst on the ground floor was housed a new glost tunnel oven along with the placers for the same, the remaining space being occupied by under - glaze printers and decorators.

This year also saw the closure of the earthenware firm of *Burgess Bros.,* of the Carlisle Works, Longton.

Dipper, with the mangle dryer for his dipped ware behind him (St. Mary's Works)

Collecting dipped ware from the mangle dryer (St. Mary's Works)

Later that year, with the onset of hostilities curtailing any further building work at the St. Mary's Works, the firm concentrated all its energy on putting existing facilities to the best use. In the first few years of the war, large quantities of Royal Albert bone china were exported to the overseas markets; in fact 1940 proved to be a record year for output at the factory.

* * *

In 1943, in recognition of the important part in which the badly depleted pottery industry was playing in the war effort, the president of the Board of Trade, the Rt. Hon. Hugh Dalton, M P., made a three day visit to the Potteries, which included an extensive tour of the St. Mary's Works.

Showrooms of Royal Albert. l to r. T E Wild, Mrs. Wallett, Mr Dalton, Sir Cecil Weir, F J Wild and Mr. A B Jones (*Grafton China*)

Mr. Dalton watches a thrower in action

Mr Dalton has a chat with some of the female workers at St. Mary's Works

It was during the war that two of T C`s grandsons performed their duty with a valour that would have made the great man himself very proud.

Firstly there was Tom's eldest son, Kenneth, who joined the Royal Artillery early in the conflict, and who, through diligence and hard work attained the rank of Captain.

Fred's eldest son, Peter, meanwhile, had joined the Royal Navy as an ordinary seaman, serving for eight months on H M S *King George V*, going with the battleship when Lord Halifax was a passenger, and later participating in the Lofoten Island raid.

Commissioned after twelve months service, he then joined Combined Operations and took part in the raid on Dieppe, and was promoted to full lieutenant.

It was while on a secret mission in the Mediterranean that he won the *Distinguished Service Cross*, the citation stating that he showed great bravery and enterprise.

Kenneth Wild, 1948

Peter G Wild D. S. C. in his Royal Navy uniform.

Gerard D Wild

Chapter Seven

Never Had It So Good

With the curtailment of the war in 1945, and the gradual return of those workers who had either volunteered or had been conscripted for active service in the defence of King and Country, things slowly returned to normal at the St. Mary's Works.

In the following year, 1946, the two Wild brothers continued their expansion programme. Again, more land to the rear of the factory was levelled, and another concrete raft was laid. This time it was for a new extension which was to house the latest type of continuous firing tunnel oven for firing *china biscuit*, thus making the St. Mary's Works an entirely *smokeless* factory.

A new showroom was also constructed; display cabinets in bird's-eye maple and recessed in Australian walnut, complete with state-of-the-art lighting, showed off the latest Royal Albert bone china to perfection

1946, showing the foundations for the new extension

On July 8th, T C Wild & Sons Ltd., St. Mary's Works offered one half of the ordinary share capital of the company for resale to the public.

The issue was for 1,500,000 ordinary shares of 1s (5p) each, at 5s 9d (28p) per share. The application lists which opened at 10.00am were closed five minutes later, by which time the shares had been subscribed *five times over.*

In a statement issued by the company, it reported that the management would be: Mr. T E Wild and Mr. F J Wild, joint managing directors, and will have associated with them as directors - Mr. Gerard D Wild, Mr. Peter G Wild D S C, Mr. Kenneth T Wild and Mr. Anthony L Wild.

For trading purposes, the subsidiary companies (namely Reid & Co., Shore & Coggins Ltd., and Chapman's (Longton) Ltd.) will be run exactly as before and will remain entirely separate from the parent company.

Anthony L Wild

On October 25th the same year, Tom Wild`s only daughter Margaret Elizabeth married Mr. John Stanier Rowley, son of Mrs. and the late Captain W J Rowley, of Stapeley Manor, Nantwich.

Margaret Elizabeth Wild and John Stanier Rowley outside Barlaston Church

* * *

Thos. C Wild & Sons Ltd., at the end of the nineteen forties, was one of the top producers of high class china tableware in the country. As well as taking great care that standards never dropped in the making of the ware, they were fortunate in having the services of a very capable and forwards looking art director: Mr. Harold Holdcroft, M.S.I.A., F.R.S.A., N.R.D.

Mr. Holdcroft had joined the firm in 1934, and as well as his role as art director, had always taken a keen interest in the factory layout.

He began as a student at Burslem School of Art, later becoming a teacher of pottery design and decoration both at Burslem and Stoke. By the late nineteen forties he was master-in-charge of Longton School of Art.

Harold Holdcroft, M S I A, F R S A, N R D.

Even though it was over forty years since the company had left the old Albert Works, there were one or two employees working at the St. Mary's Works who had started their career at the old factory.

There was the works engineer, Mr. E Rigby, there was the head glost placer, Mr. J Worsdale - both could boast of having served over forty three years with the firm, and then there was Mr. Frederick Baker, 71 years old and head turner at the firm since 1904.

Born in Longton in 1878, he was ten years old when he started as a part-time mould runner at one of Longton`s many china factories. When he was twelve and a half he commenced his apprenticeship, and for many months received a weekly wage of ten shillings (50p). He became a journeyman at the old Albert Works at the age of 18 in 1896.

In April 1949, the *`Pottery Gazette and Glass Trade Review`* interviewed Mr. Baker, this is a little of that article:

'Fred has witnessed a gradual improvement in working conditions, wages and amenities. One of the outstanding developments connected with the turner's craft is the comparatively recent introduction of the tungsten-tipped cutter. Just how important this has been can be judged from the fact that there was once a time when the turner's lunch hour was made up as follows: 15 minutes for eating and 45 minutes for filing (sharpening) his cutter. Happily this practice has long since been discontinued. Another objectionable practice was the charging of 6d (2 1/2p) a week for gas-lighting, 4d (2p) a week for sweeping, and 2d (1p) a week for the privilege of using the toilet!

Fred has been one of the firm's most regular and punctual workers. He has rarely been ill - and then only for odd days at a time. He is a pipe smoker.

"I never smoke on the factory," said Fred; *"at least, I have not since I was 25,"* he added.

"How was that Fred?" we asked.

"It happened like this," said Fred. *"The late Mr. T C Wild once caught me smoking in the lavatory. He told me that I had never seen him smoking on the works, and I was never likely to. He was very pleasant about it, and advised me to leave my pipe at home as it set a bad example to the rest of the men. From that day to this I have never smoked on the works."*

Football enthusiasts will be interested to learn that Fred's son is the well known professional footballer, Frank Baker, who plays at inside-left for the Stoke City F C first team.'

Mr. Frederick Baker

Mr. E Rigby and Mr. J Worsdale

The famous American entertainer, the late Danny Kaye, during a visit to the St. Mary's Works, 1949

* * *

As the country got back to normal after the six long years of war, the British people began to shake off their mood of sombre seriousness, and started to re-learn how to enjoy themselves once again.

And probably nowhere was this more apparent than in the Potteries, where the workpeople have always had an almost fanatical attitude to enjoying themselves - they work hard, and play hard. Although at this time - the late forties and early fifties - wartime rationing was still in force, and thus limiting some extent the wherewithal to enjoy oneself, the hard-working potter would grab any and every opportunity to 'have a good time'.

One such opportunity, and one that was eagerly anticipated, and meticulously planned for, was the firm's annual day-trip to the sea-side - and what made it even better for these financially challenged workers, was that it was actually paid for by their employers!

Most of the pottery companies would arrange, and pay for, their staff and workers to have a day out, either at the sea-side, or to places of interest. Even the smallest of firms usually managed at least one day-trip during the summer months.

For the T C Wild`s group of companies, with their large workforces, this meant a great deal of planning and a not inconsiderable amount of expenditure (although it was more than likely that this was offset against their tax bill).

The most popular destinations for the potter's 'day-outs' were the North Wales resorts of Rhyl and Llandudno, plus Blackpool, and the now almost forgotten resort of New Brighton. All these places, it will be noted, are within two or three hours drive of the Potteries, for it was usually by motor-coach that they all travelled - with the bigger companies hiring as many as four large coaches - and picking everyone up outside the works entrance.

For the smaller firms, there was always the closer, but nonetheless very attractive destinations of Alton Towers and Trentham Gardens.

Royal Standard workers with Kenneth Wild about to leave for Blackpool. 1949

Chapman`s workers ready to board the coach for New Brighton.1950
Note the lorry leaving the entrance to the Albert Works

T C Wilds` workers with Tom and Kenneth Wild, outside the St.Mary's Works, waiting for the coach to take them to Llandudno. 1950

T C Wild's workers and staff arriving at Blackpool, 1949.
In the centre of the group are Tom Wild and Anthony Wild

Pleasure Beach at Blackpool

Pavilion Gardens, Rhyl

New Brighton

Lord Street, Southport

Alton Towers

Trentham Gardens

The Miniature Railway, Trentham Gardens, Staffs. P.4

Miniature Railway, Trentham Gardens

* * *

As the nineteen fifties got under way, T C Wild & Sons Ltd. began their largest expansion programme yet. The St. Mary's Works were about to double in size.

In March 1951, the old council school adjoining the St. Mary's Works on the eastern side was demolished (this school, incidentally, was the one that both Tom and Fred Wild had attended as youngsters), and immediately work was started on the construction of a large extension which would house the new canteen, finished warehouses, new administration block and showrooms.

By December of that year, the steel framework for the extension was in place, and a stone-laying ceremony took place when the joint managing directors, T. E .Wild and F. J. Wild did the honours.

The old council school has to go.

Tom and Fred Wild lay the commemorative stone in memory of their father Thomas Clark Wild; J.P.....In the centre of the picture is a young Patrick Wild, the great grandson of the founder.

The steel frame goes up.

The new board room. From left to right are Fred J. Wild, Tom E. Wild, Ken Wild & Anthony Wild.

In the summer of 1952, after further work on the extension, which included the installation of a third electric enamel kiln along with an ultra-modern sliphouse and packing department, the new extension was up and running.

Thos E. Wild and Fred J. Wild in their office.

The new Works Canteen

By the end of the year, the extra output that was now available was put to good use when the factory embarked on the production of 'Coronation Ware', ready for the new Queen's inauguration planned for June of the following year.

Two operatives at the St. Mary's Works with a selection of Coronation mugs and beakers

At Thos. C. Wild and Sons, Ltd.

Preparing for the Christmas Party - T C Wild`s

Chapter Eight

The End of an Era

The nineteen sixties began with the T C Wild group of companies leading the field in the bone china industry. The output from their four main factories was tremendous - no other pottery company in Longton came near to them as regards to sales, whether at home or abroad.

In 1960, T C Wild & Sons Ltd. took over the well known *'Paragon China'*. This company, which was first established in 1897 by Herbert James Aynsley, John Gerrard Aynsley and William Illingworth, started life as 'Star China', and in 1919 became known as 'Paragon China' under the control of Hugh Irving and his father-in-law Herbert James Aynsley, when it was named after Star China's most popular product.

Paragon China was acknowledged as being one of the finest producers of bone china in the country.

In a statement, T C Wilds` announced that they had acquired the whole of the issued share capital of 'Paragon China Ltd', and that it would continue to operate as a wholly-owned subsidiary of T C Wild & Sons Ltd.

Mr Hugh Irving (left) with his two sons, Guy Irving and Leslie Irving.
This photograph was taken in 1945 on the return of Guy Irving from a prisoner-of-war camp in Germany, where he had spent the last five years.

The same year (1960) saw Peter G Wild, managing director of 'Shore & Coggins' appointed as a Justice of the Peace.

* * *

Mr. Fred J Wild

In January of the following year, Fred Wild died at his home in Rhos-on-Sea at the age of 68. In his obituary, much was made of his enterprise and his technical expertise, quoting most notably, his introduction of the first gas-fired biscuit tunnel oven to be used in Longton for bone china.

* * *

FOUR GENERATIONS AT ST. MARY'S WORKS
Patrick Wild (right) is the son of Mr. Kenneth Wild (left). Seated in the middle is his grandfather, Mr. Thomas E Wild the 70 year old chairman. Overlooking them all is the portrait of the founder, Thomas Clark Wild himself.

When he joined the staff of the St. Mary's Works in May 1961, Mr Patrick Wild became the first member of the fourth generation of the Wild family to enter the firm of T C Wild & Sons Ltd.

* * *

The patterns now being produced at the St.Mary's Works were, and still are, very popular. Many of these patterns have become almost household names - *Moss Rose, Lenora, Val d'ore*, and of course, the most popular of them all - ***Old Country Roses*** (which was originally to be called Treasure Garden).

As well as producing so much well potted and beautifully decorated bone china, the company went even further in ensuring customer loyalty, by guaranteeing to be able to replace any pattern for the subsequent twenty years.

* * *

Pottery Queen Selected

The Pottery Queen for 1964 was Miss Edna Newnes, a gilder from Thos. C Wild & Sons Ltd. She was selected from finalists at a ball in Trentham Gardens.

JACOBEAN

2554

Engraved design printed in Burnt Umber and enamelled by hand
A blaze of colour with translucent Turquoise predominant

THOS. C. WILD & SONS LTD., LONGTON, STOKE-ON-TRENT, ENGLAND

'Jacobean' by Royal Albert. 1948

Miss Yolande Donlan admiring 'Royal Albert Bone China' which is featured in the film 'Mr. Drake's Duck' with Douglas Fairbanks

Kind permission Angel Productions

THOS. C. WILD & SONS LTD., LONGTON, STOKE-ON-TRENT, ENGLAND

Advertisement for 1951

ROYAL ALBERT

Bone China

Elfin

A delightfully pleasing design. The centre motif is in soft pinks, greys and greens and the ground in Turquoise. Elfin is on Lyric shape and has a gold finish

THOS. C. WILD & SONS LTD ST. MARY'S CHINA WORKS STOKE-ON-TRENT ENGLAND

'Elfin' by Royal Albert. 1960

THOS. C. WILD & SONS LTD · LONGTON · STOKE-ON-TRENT · ENGLAND

'Brigadoon' by Royal Albert. 1963

Nymph

A CHARMING ARRANGEMENT OF
GRASSES AND SEEDHEADS IN
GREENS, BROWNS AND RUST WITH
A MATCHING SOLID COLOUR

Designed by Joyce Storey

QUEEN ANNE CHINA

GREENDOCK ST · LONGTON · STOKE-ON-TRENT

'Nymph' by Shore & Coggins.1963

'Leonora' by Royal Albert. 1964

QUEEN ANNE CHINA

Shore & Coggins Ltd., Greendock St., Longton, Stoke-on-Trent, Room 339 Imperial Hotel

FOR THOSE WHO USE THEIR COFFEE SETS, QUEEN ANNE INTRODUCE CROW
COFFEE WARE WITH LARGER COFFEE POTS AND TEACUP SIZE COFFEE CUP

'Crown Coffee Ware' by Shore & Coggins. 1964

'Old Country Roses' by Royal Albert. 1964

'Val D'or' by Royal Albert. 1964

'Keepsake' by Royal Albert. 1964

'Heritage' by Royal Albert. 1964

'Lavender Rose' by Royal Albert. 1964

Connoiseur

an AP product

THOS. C. WILD & SONS LTD · LONGTON · STOKE-ON-TRENT · ENGLAND

'Connoiseur' by Royal Albert. 1966

ROYAL ALBERT
Bone China
ENGLAND

THOS. C. WILD & SONS LTD · LONGTON · STOKE-ON-TRENT · ENGLAND

'Winsome' by Royal Albert. 1966

Allied English Potteries

T C Wild & Sons Ltd merged with the Lawley Group in July 1964. It was a merger that signalled the way the pottery industry in the UK was heading - it was the time for the BIG concerns to forge ahead.

The Lawley Group started life in 1908 when Tom and Edgar Lawley established a retail company in Birmingham. Incorporated as Lawleys (1921) Ltd., and later renamed as Lawleys Ltd., in 1929, it was run by Edgar alone after 1936 when he bought out Tom's share of the business.

In 1940 they began to acquire controlling interests in Stoke-on-Trent's pottery companies. *'North Staffordshire Pottery Company'* was the first of their acquisitions, and by 1948 they had controlling interests in a further 10 companies, including: *Adderleys Ltd., Barlows (Longton) Ltd., Garfield Pottery Ltd., and Hughes (Fenton) Ltd.*

In 1952 the company was taken over by S Pearson & Son Ltd., and in 1964 merged with T C Wild & Sons Ltd. The resulting giant was renamed *Allied English Potteries.*

In a statement made in July 1964, it was stated that Thos. C. Wild & Sons Ltd., would retain their identity, with Mr. T. E. Wild, present chairman, invited to become first life president. Remaining directors would continue in office, with Mr. P. G. Wild and Mr. K. T. Wild invited to join the board of Lawley. Lord Poole, Lawley chairman, would be appointed chairman of Wilds'

T C Wild & Sons Ltd., would continue to operate as a separate entity, as would Pearson's other recent acquisition, *'Royal Crown Derby Porcelain Company'.*

Lord Snowdon watching a plate maker at work, during a visit to the St. Mary's Works in 1966

Managing director Kenneth Wild, being interviewed by Mr. Bertram Mycock, BBC industrial editor for the television feature 'Made in Britain.' 1966

Mr Harold Holdcroft, art director, showing the new pattern, 'Centennial Rose' to Mr Jack McIntyre, president of the Rotary Club of Montreal-Lakeshore. The original rose, which the new Royal Albert pattern copied, was grown and selected to celebrate Canada's Centennial. Also in the picture are Kenneth and Patrick Wild.

On October 5th 1968, the life president, Tom E Wild was killed in a car crash at Barlaston, a little village just outside the Potteries. The last of the second generation of Wilds had gone.

* * *

In November 1971, S Pearson & Sons Ltd., owners of Allied English Potteries acquired *'Doulton & Company'*.

In July the following year, the companies merged, and in January of 1973 the company was renamed *'Royal Doulton Tableware Limited'*.

There was to be no more 'T C Wild & Sons Ltd.'

It was the end of an era!

A Sad Sight
The gates at the rear of St. Mary's Works - holding back the remains of the once mighty factory. (2002)

The famous monogram that adorned the gates - T C W & S

Backstamps

Royal Albert

Thomas C Wild.....pre 1904

Thomas C Wild.....1904 - 1907

Thomas C Wild.....1907 - 1922

Thomas C Wild.....1917+

Thomas C Wild.....1917+

Thomas C Wild.....1920+

Thomas C Wild.....1927+

Thomas C Wild.....1935

Thomas C Wild.....1935

Thomas C Wild.....1959+

This small plate was issued to all managers in 1959

Reid & Co

Reid & Co.....1913

Reid & Co.....1922+

Reid & Co.....1924+

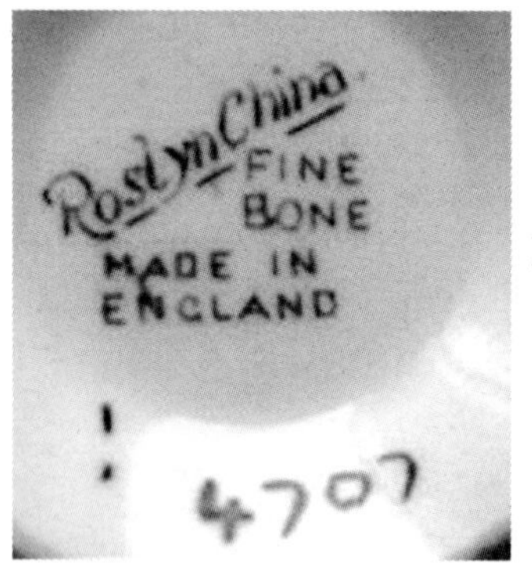

Reid & Co.....1937+

Reid & Co.....1937 - 1946

Shore & Coggins

Shore & Coggins.....1911+

Shore & Coggins.....1922+

Shore & Coggins.....1930+

Shore & Coggins.....1936 - 1966

Shore & Coggins.....1949

Shore & Coggins.....1950

Shore & Coggins.....1959+

Shore & Coggins.....1959+

Chapman, Longton, Ltd

Chapman's.....1916 - 1930

Chapman's.....c1920

Chapman's.....1930 - 1949

Chapman's.....1938 - 1941

Chapman's.....1949+

Chapman's.....1949+

T W Barlow & Sons

T W Barlow & Sons.....c1900

T W Barlow & Sons.....1928 - 1936

T W Barlow & Sons.....1936 - 1940

Wild Bros

Wild Bros.....c1904

Wild Bros.....1904+

Wild Bros.....1922 - 1927

William Lowe

William Lowe 1874 - 1912

William Lowe.....c1900

William Lowe.....1912+

William Lowe.....1928+

Burgess Bros

Burgess Bros.....1922 - 1939

Burgess Bros.....1922 - 1939

Blair & Co

Blair & Co.....1900+

Wild & Adams

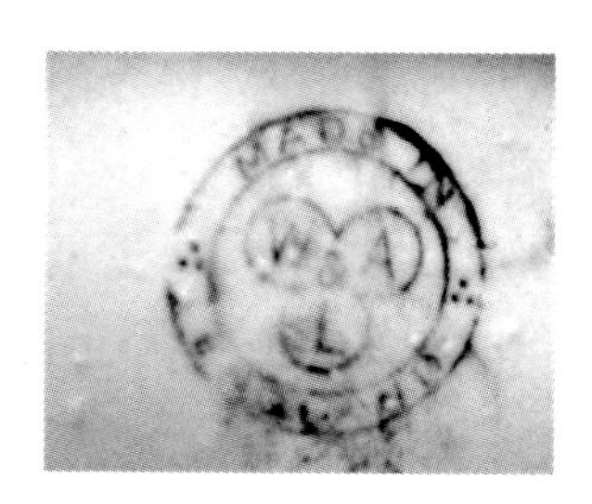

Wild & Adams.....c1909

Wild & Adams.....1909 - 1927

Wild & Adams.....1923 - 1927

Thomas Cone.....1935+

The Wares

The following photographs show just a few of the many thousands of patterns produced by the Wild group over the seventy five years that they were operating.

Wild & Adams (earthenware) c1909. 12½ in high

Thos. C Wild 'Nevis' 1905

Thos. C Wild c1910

Thos. C Wild c1920. Stamped in 22ct Gold

A typical ‘Derby’ cup made by Thos. C Wild

Chapmans, Longton, Ltd. c1916

Chapmans, Longton, Ltd. c1950

Chapmans, Longton, Ltd. c1920

Sugar & Cream to match the above

Chapmans, Longton, Ltd. 1950s. (Falling Leaf)

Chapmans, Longton, Ltd.

Shore & Coggins c1936

Shore & Coggins c1936

Shore & Coggins c1940

Shore & Coggins c1950

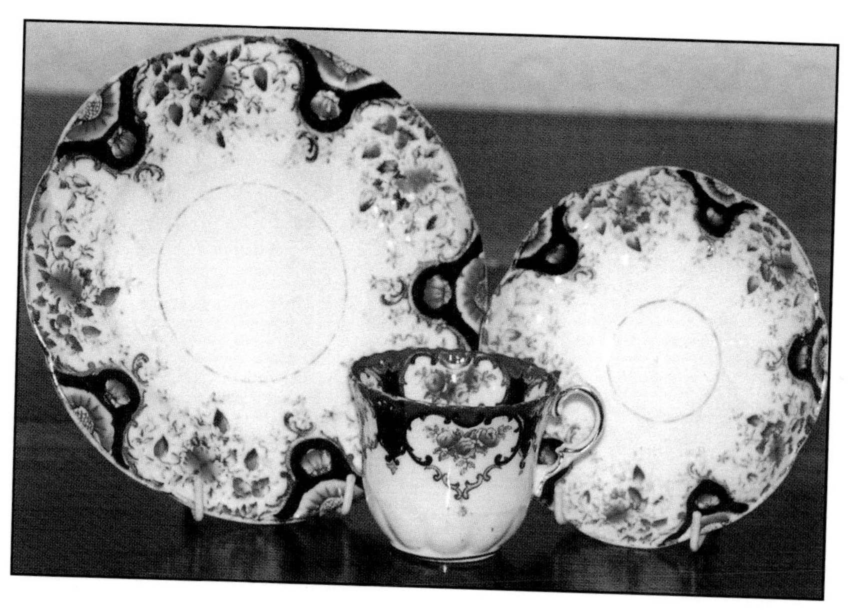

Wild Bros. c1904

Wild Bros. (Prim) c1904

Wild Bros. (Bon). 1922 - 1927

Reid & Co (Lily) c1937

Reid & Co. c1937

William Lowe c1900

William Lowe 1928 - 1930

William Lowe (Kiang) 1930s

Thos. Cone Ltd (Alma Ware) 1937

T W Barlow & Son Ltd (Coronation Ware) 'Balmoral'. Early 1900s

Old Country Roses

Old Country Roses

Old Country Roses

OLD COUNTRY ROSES